UNL YOUR FAMILY

G000077410

Chaos to Creativity
in One Week

Second Edition

Ben Crawford

PRESS

Bellevue, KY

FFT Press
Bellevue, KY

AUTHOR'S NOTE: All specific words and medical references related to current times have been removed to comply with Amaon's guidelines.

Front Cover Photo by Dove Crawford @doveskyhigh

ISBN: 9798635926680

This book is dedicated to

Kami, Dove, Eden, Seven, Memory, Filia & Rainier.

That was one hell of a week.

PREFACE TO THE SECOND EDITION

I set out to write this book mostly as a personal challenge. The book's topic included writing the book itself which made things very difficult towards the end when I was writing about things as they happened and I wasn't sure how they were going to turn out. This is why I wrote the book predominantly in 4 days, published it on google docs, never got a proofread, and never considered getting it printed to paperback.

Less than 4 days later 2,700 people had downloaded it and 71 people had rated it an average of 4.9 stars.

It rocketed to:
- #1 Best Seller in Personal Transformation
- #1 New Release in Time Management and Business
- #1 New Release in Two-Hour Parenting and Relationship Short Reads
- #2 Best Seller in Personal Transformation
- #4 Best Seller in Parenting

Most important to me I started hearing stories from readers.

On the phone from Steve, I heard: "I got more done on my first day than I did in 6 months!"

On reviews I read:

"Right to the point, short, practical. I downloaded it, finished it in one hour and knew what I wanted to change. The next day I felt more energy to be productive." - Tatjana K.

"Very inspiring read! We had our first goals meeting yesterday and today we're following our schedule." - Ben J. Bishop

And finally:

"Stop scrolling like a mad bastard and read this book!" - Madison

And that was all in the first week.

My conclusions:

1. The things I recommend in this book work.
2. I should proofread this book.
3. A paperback would be nice.

So thank you for everyone who downloaded and rated in that first week. Here is the slightly revised AND edited version.

- Ben

INTRO

Action expresses priorities.

-        *- Mahatma Gandhi*

Most of our lives are run off of panic. These scary times just reveal the truths that have been there all along. When you live a life responding to the stimuli provided to you by the news, the culture, or your boss you will live an unsatisfied life. It can feel impossible to change. There is only one way we have found. And it works for adults and kids. It is to fill your life with the things that give you purpose. When you fill your life with purpose, not only do you get results of what purpose creates (art, new skill sets, money), but you will find that you do not have as much time and energy for the panic that used to consume you. We have spent the last 20 years living unconventionally. We lived off of welfare and we have been millionaires. We've worked from home, got a nursing degree we never used, quit school altogether, spent 6 months walking, and lived a year with no rules. So, when we hear on the news that the world is in crisis, we saw an opportunity, maybe, even a challenge. My hope is that you neither copy us nor write us off. That you see us as fellow travelers and are moved to see your own world through a new lens. I hope this book provokes change in your family. If you take one additional step, in a direction of your choosing from reading this, consider it a success. This book is intended to be read in less than 60 minutes. It is intended to create immediate action. It is intended to give you more of what you want. If you're open to that…

Let's go!

SATURDAY

PANIC

On March 22nd, 2020 the Governor of Ohio declared that the entire state was on lockdown. This came after weeks of school, restaurants and bars closing. Life as we knew it was over. Online, a new culture had developed. 99% of the news and social media were talking about the same global disaster. It was the same things being said in a bunch of different ways. Things are closing, this is scary, stay home. The amount of time spent on the news or social media did not increase the amount that you would learn, it just increased the number of times you would go through the same loop.

Things are closing, this is scary, stay home.

Things are closing, this is scary, stay home.

Things are closing, this is scary, stay home.

While true, this loop was no longer helpful for our family. All these questions did was keep our minds and bodies in a state of panic that we had become addicted to. Our life became an exercise in repeating them online, in our conversations, and in our heads.

The lockdown brought to the surface the underlying panic that had existed long before and controls our lives in many undesirable ways. Panic asks the questions: "How can I survive?" Panic says, "I'm going to miss out, if I don't keep checking for updates!" The problem with panic is that it causes you to dwell on these loops and repeat them again and again. The problem with panic wasn't the information. It was the redundancy of the information without any helpful action.

As a family, we had already determined our course of action. We were stuck at home. Everything was closed. The continual stream of information was not doing anything to change that. But the information was still addictive. It fed our lizard brain. The part of our brain that prioritized survival and said the world was out to get you. The fight or flight, the fear, and the temporary relief that at least I'm doing *something*. The cycle gave us an artificial sense of control. The problem was, after hours of spending time on the cycle we were the same people. We were in the same situation. Nothing had changed.

Similar loops had occurred in other areas of my life. I had a loop where I could check my email, check Facebook for notifications, check Youtube for comments, views, and revenue, and then go back to checking email. I could do the whole thing in 20 seconds as long as there weren't any snags but the problem was not in the length of time it took. The problem was the number of times I would do it. Multiple times an hour, hundreds of times a day. And at the end of the day I had nothing to show for it. If you were to keep track of it, it would look something like this

7 - 8:00   Wake up, enter in Social Media Panic Loop
8 - 9:00   Breakfast while looking at social media
9 - 10:00   Try to sort out which tasks feel most urgent
10- 12   Work on tasks while checking FB, IG, email, and NEWS every 15 min
12 -1:00   Lunch
1 - 4:00   Work on more tasks distractedly while checking FB, IG, NEWS every 15 min.
4 - 6:00   Completely burn out, give self permission to veg on Netflix, FB, IG, NEWS
6 - 7:00   Dinner
7 - 11:00   Completely veg on Netflix, FB, IG, NEWS
11:00   Crash into bed feeling exhausted and accomplishing little

Start over again the next day feeling fat, powerless, and like your dreams are slipping away, day by day, never to be fulfilled.

Instead of the standard YouTube drama and sports highlights there were repeating loops of global catastrophe. Different content, same result.

When we turn our eyes to social media, we are letting other people decide what we are going to think about. It's been well documented over the years how powerful Facebook's algorithms are and the marketing psychology and manipulation they employ to use us to accomplish their goals to make money. It turns out, likes and hearts have far less to do with me and my friends and more to do with what's going to put more dollars in Facebook's bank account. Their goal as a platform is not to "connect" me and my friends but to prey off of my insecurities in order to make money for their shareholders.

Every time I logged into social media there were infinite rabbit holes of conversations that it was impossible to avoid. In the hiking community that we are involved in, the big discussion was whether or not people should stay on the Appalachian Trail who had started a Thru Hike.

People were passionate on either side. Some saying it was completely selfish to stay on trail and anyone who stayed was an asshole. People on the other side said, hikers are in the woods and the small towns along the trail want the money and besides, everyone that was "going home" is really just going out to the trails to hike during the day anyways. I had a lot to add to these never ending streams of conversations. But I couldn't figure out if anyone was reading my responses and actually changing their mind. Was I writing those posts for just myself?

Things are closing, this is scary, stay home.

Participating in all of these forms of social panic were ways of giving control of my day over to others. The earlier in the day I started, the earlier I gave my control over. I could open up Facebook while still on my pillow and feel rage, confusion, terror, and laugh at memes. While each of these may be based upon truth, none of these things would have been my desired purpose, if you would have asked me the night before. Now they had set the course of my day, and I hadn't even got out of bed.

At this point, I will pause and say that while this book is being written during a global quarantine and being used as a primary example, I have spent a lifetime observing various other activities that fill this same void during times of peacefulness. School and work are the two biggest ones that can create a sense of panic and fill our life continually. There are many others. Buying new stuff to keep up with the Joneses, micromanaging kids activities based on fear, and getting a mortgage on a bigger house we can't afford, are just a few examples. There are many micro activities that bring this sense of panic on an hourly basis. Compulsively checking the weather, stock prices, email, twitter, Instagram, Facebook, or anything else that has notifications. In your life this is how you sort them: Panic loops demand immediate attention and produce zero positive long term results.

Getting involved in drama cycles is an easy way to avoid the things that are most important. The things I do care about. The things I want to be known for and the things I want to remember later on in my life. But how could we stop? EVERYONE was talking about Corona, even my wife and 6 kids! We have 8 devices in our house that access the internet, most of them we carry around in our pocket.

That night my wife, Kami and I went to bed burned out. This had been going on for a few weeks with no signs of letting up. We were burned out from social media, burned out from the same loops going round and round in our head. We were burned out from feeling like victims that were caught in a cycles completely outside of our control. We lay in bed and restarted a series we had watched years ago: HBO's Westworld. It seemed like our only option to find relief from the cycle.

Through counseling I had learned, "what you resist, persists." Want proof?

Try *NOT* to think about a pink elephant?

What are you thinking about right now?

….a pink elephant.

The more I tell you not to, the more you will. So, the more we would try NOT to fixate on the panic, the *more* we would fixate on the panic. We needed a tool more powerful than resistance. Something more powerful than discipline.

What could that be?

I'm glad you asked.

SUNDAY

PURPOSE

Purpose is doing something, anything, with intention. Because *you* want to. Because *you* value it. Because *you* decided it. What do you want to do?

Often, we get sucked into panic loops, not because we actually want to, but because it's easiest. Here's how I know the difference. How do you feel after one hour of an activity? How do you feel after one week? How do you anticipate feeling after a lifetime? No one wants it to be said at their funeral that they *liked* the best memes, left the best comments, and scrolled like a mad bastard without ever giving up. These activities are reactive. They are fillers. They are the corn syrup of our diet. We should tolerate them but not build our life around them.

Living a life of purpose is better than living in a state of reactive panic. The only way we have found to move beyond the panic is to fill our lives with purpose. Something we can care about more. When you fill your life with fulfilling purpose it will push the panic out. You won't have time for it. This is a win/win. Almost too good to be true. While the gratification with purpose is delayed, there is *more* of it. So, not only do you get the gratification you desire, you leave behind much of the stress with which the panic was filling your life.

Do you know who makes money off of your panic? Large corporations. Yet, a number of people have made a lot of money stepping into their purpose. Imagine if Steve Jobs or Mark Zuckerberg had spent their best hours *scrolling* like mad bastards?

Panic asks the question: *How can I survive?* Purpose asks the question: *What do I want and how do I want to get there?* While most of the safety decisions around the corona virus was outside of our control (besides staying home and washing hands - activities that literally took less than 5 minutes a day), having the best week ever or possible is completely within our control. We can make all sorts of decisions that determine whether we are going to work towards our goals or desires by reading a book, watching a youtube video, or learning a new skill. Not saying that having control makes the decisions easy (see "Resistance" in Steven Pressfield's War of Art), but they have a result that I can take ownership in and work to change if I don't like it.

Now, that we've agreed it's better to live with purpose instead of panic, let's talk about how the hell you do that when you're submerged in a culture all around you in a state of panic.

FAMILY

For the last 5 years, Kami and I had been having a weekly business meeting to discuss family goals and logistics. When I worked in corporate jobs serving clients like Google and Facebook, I learned that leadership meetings were a valuable time to create vision, communicate problems, and come up with solutions that could be implemented to the entire organization. Every successful business and organization had space for planning and intentional decision making that involved collaboration and cooperation. The good shit didn't happen by accident. This is no less true in families.

As Kami and I were going through the corona news cycle (things are closing, this is scary, stay home), we could see that our kids had developed cycles of their own. The feelings of being trapped at home and having all of their activities canceled had created this void that they were filling with whatever was easiest. Movies on Netflix, video games, sleeping in, and memes were filling their day, too. So, the stakes were high for us. If we couldn't figure out how to transition to purpose, how should I expect our 6 kids to make the move? If we couldn't figure out a transition to something better, we could be looking forward to months of panic loops, not just weeks.

In the book E-myth, I had read that successful entrepreneurs work *on* their business not *in* their business. This means they take the time to consistently pull back from the day to day grind (panic loop) to assess the entire system and make tweaks on a level that will consistently and systematically change the results. It was working smarter not harder. For us, we had had our weekly family biz meeting at a fun breakfast spot that we enjoyed. This helped with motivation when we just weren't "feeling it." Now, with all the restaurants closed, our dining room table would have to do. For those that are trying this out for the first time, I would recommend something that makes it special. It could be coffee, alcohol, or even a fancy chocolate bar. Anything that can pull you out of the grind of living, parenting, or business.

For the single parent or solo individual: The mindset of purpose we're discussing can be done alone in writing, with a partner or friend. Physical location is key. Even if you're stick at home, you can choose a spot in you home or outside where you wouldn't normally meet. The point is to step away from the stress of your everyday life and see the direction you are heading. Then you can decide if it's something you like, or brainstorm what it would take to change.

I told Kami of my concern and of the vision I had for something that could be better. It started something like, "I don't like the direction our family is heading, but we have an incredible opportunity. I think we could have an amazing week accomplishing some goals and learning about ourselves." We have learned that in order to live a life of purpose you must first learn to live a week of purpose. The best tool to manage time is a schedule. Kami and I started with me jotting down my thoughts on a piece of paper, a rough draft schedule of how I thought we could run the week. Kami could then communicate how that worked or didn't work for her, including did it meet her needs and did she think it would work for the kids from her point of view.

A schedule provides a default for our time.
Many of us who are used to schedules being imposed upon us by others (clients, bosses, schools) see a schedule as a prison. That's unfortunate because a schedule is just a tool that we can use for our own goals, not just someone else's. It's an expressed desire that you have to do something and a plan to make that happen. It's saying, unless something better comes along, this is what I plan on doing. It's a way to counter the alternative panic loops that will always seem easier in the moment. Just like stocking healthier food in your pantry makes it easier to eat healthy when you have a weak moment, having a schedule lined up of things *you* value will be easier when your brain is fried and you want to veg. Having a schedule does *not* mean you HAVE to do it. It just means if you want to do it, you won't have to plan for it in the moment. While creating a schedule, I can be very intentional about how I want to use my time, and then when I'm being drawn into a perspective of panic, following the schedule keeps me intentional.

A schedule is a budget for your time. When you have limited money creating a budget helps. You make a one time decision about a budget which helps with the micro spending decisions that come up throughout the day. Our time is more limited than our money. A schedule is a way of planning your values. It is better to make these decisions from a state of sanity and purpose instead of the impulsive decisions from the lizard brain. If not, we will click down rabbit holes only to come up for air hours later and ask "what the hell just happened?" Our schedule reflects *our* family's values. Some events are natural (like watching movies together). Some have been accumulated (like running). Your schedule should reflect *your* values. Walking, meditation, coffee and reading, a hot bath… the list is endless. You can literally schedule anything! Some people feel silly scheduling their values because they don't think they are important. This is NOT the time to be judging the importance of your values. Just accept them. Any value that is expressed through purpose will be better than reacting to a panic loop created by someone else.

When Kami and I came up with our first family schedule 12 years ago, it felt extremely claustrophobic, restrictive and scary. Now we are on our 100th iteration and we have been creating schedules as a family for years; scheduling workouts, movies, and even our sex life.

Kami wanted to see more of what I had in mind so I showed her a rough schedule that I had scribbled out on a legal pad. This schedule was intended for the whole family so it needed to have enough structure to keep us all on track but it also needed to provide enough freedom for individuals to thrive. After all, we were dealing with ages 9 - 40. I knew that each of the kids would use these work blocks differently, and we would figure that out later, but we needed to start with a structure we could all agree to, if this was going to work in one house. If you're solo I'm confident these tools will work for you. If you're a part of a family, a group, a schedule becomes imperative. For a group that shares a space and resources our schedule has become our number one tool to express our values.

For some this will feel like working in reverse. It is very common to create a goal and then create the way to get there. Carving out this space/time, for us, felt like opening up windows of opportunity that inspired us to dream about the goals we could fill it with, but more on that later.

Monday thru Friday

7:15 - 7:50am	Group Workout
8:00 - 9:00	Breakfast/Quiet Time
9:00 - 10:00	Individual Work Block 1
10:00 - 10:15	Break
10:15 - 11:15	Individual Work Block 2
11:15 - 11:30	Break
11:30 - 12:30	Individual Work Block 3
12:30 - 1:15	Lunch
1:15 - 2:15	Individual Work Block 4
2:15 - 4:00	Break
4:00 - 5:30	Group Running
6:00 - 7:00	Dinner
8:00 - 9:00	One Episode of TV series
10:00	Go to bed

We are not used to seeing schedules like this for the home, so it may feel weird but it shouldn't be. Schedules are very common in other areas of our life. School schedules are much more strict, and work schedules are jam packed with meetings and deadlines. Elon Musk schedules his day in 5 minute increments.

I felt like this schedule was a great place to start. The goal of a good schedule is not to *fill* every minute of the day. The point is that you are *prioritizing* your values in your day. You're saying, these things *first*. You can start by scheduling one or two things that are important to you. You can always cancel if something more important comes up. But if you don't come up with a plan of purpose, your time will be filled with reactive panic cycles. If you don't come up with your own schedule, you will be living out someone else's.

Creating a schedule in a family, prioritizes opportunities for our breaks to be at the same time, to feel energized knowing we were all on a mission, to support each other, and to create times to connect and do things together that we value.

For someone who has a busy life, filled with commitments, this process becomes more important, *not* less. Everyone has free time. For some it's an hour, for other's it's 15 minutes. How you prioritize your 15 minutes will determine how you spend your days if they ever become free. Many use the amount of time they have free as an excuse but it's often lack of prioritization that keeps people from ever having enough time.

I shared with Kami the schedule I had drafted and she had some immediate feedback.

1. She had concerns about the cleanliness of the house and chores getting done, if our time was filled with work blocks, and immediately expressed that she would feel much better if our schedule included this.

2. She also suggested that we have a time daily where we can check in and evaluate how things were going with the kids. A place to connect and make sure everyone was doing ok with all of the changes.

3. But, she liked the overall idea and was very supportive

One of the keys to working together as a leadership team has been seeing our differences as an asset, not a liability. Kami's values reflect, not only her values, but values in many of our kids. They are very different from mine and also reflect blindspots that I have in my personality. I am much more adventurous and inventive, and love new horizons, and impossible goals. She loves comfort and relaxing environments. We have learned that it doesn't need to be either/or. If a schedule is going to be successful for all of us, it needs to embrace both of these perspectives.

So, even though it would be nicer to hear "great job, looks like you already pumped out a masterpiece," I've learned it's best to present something like it's a rough draft - open to feedback.

The first result of her feedback was we created a chore time at 3pm. Instead of having the dishes immediately done after breakfast and lunch, which was Kami's preference, she was willing to compromise knowing it was scheduled later. We also added an intentional conversation time to our dinner. This would be a time where we could hear back from the kids. Normally we didn't have much structure in our house and we know that everyone deals with change differently. We wanted the ability to makes changes on the spot if we needed to and this would be the best way to hear how they were doing on a consistent basis. At the dinner table we would start off with some simple questions to kickstart the conversation:

- What was your high point of the day?
- What was your low point of the day?
- How do you feel?

These would be open ended questions with no feedback (or cross-talk) permitted. This protected the kids and meant, as parents, this would just be a time for listening. Our kids are willing to share more when they know they're not going to get advice after their story.

There are times and places for advice. Early on in our parenting we gave advice often. But we found that much of it was not effective. The kids were not hearing it. They were not internalizing it. Our conclusion was that most the advice we were giving was for us to feel better instead of what was in the kids best interests. With kids, it doesn't matter if you're right if you're not heard. While it felt counter-productive we found that often it was best to just listen. Just like you would a friend. What started to happen was that our kids started to come to us for advice. And when they did we knew they were far more likely to appreciate and implement our words.

Creating spaces that are focused on listening instead of fixing also allowed us parents to be honest about our struggles and successes instead of feeling like we needed to be a hero or example. I know this type of parenting is not natural for some and if it seems impossible, keep on reading.

At this point, we both felt good about the schedule knowing that this was a trial period and we would re-evaluate after a week.

But now, the most crucial step was ahead of us. Getting the kids on board.

THE PITCH

If we were going to run a schedule for the entire house, we needed to have everyone in agreement. With 6 kids who had no idea of our plans that meant 75% of our population still needed convincing. "The Pitch" is not just a catchy title, it can be a life-changing reality.

It contrasts with the way we used to parent, which is by *telling* our kids what is happening. This section could have been titled "The Announcement." Announcements create a sense of powerlessness. They say, "this has already been decided and you don't have a choice." Many parenting models are based on the idea that the role of a parent is to decide what is best for their child and then enforce it. While I'm not completely opposed to this model, especially at young ages, we have found many weaknesses with it.

1. It does not result in kids taking ownership of the goals or values of the parents.

2. It results in relational strain with parents having to act as cops and constantly enforce their values.

3. Kids become more focused on consequences of parents as opposed to the values being taught.

4. It results in kids wanting to escape being controlled.

5. It teaches a system of using power (and often violence) to transfer values.

We practiced these models for almost two decades. The results of using power to force our will upon our kids was great for short-term results but bad for long-term change. We want to prioritize long term relationship and that means learning a new way to transfer values.

Over the years, as our spiritual and relational understanding has changed we have also adopted more humility in our parenting models by accepting that maybe we don't know what's best for each of our children at any given time. Each of our kids is unique, and they are being raised at a time that is different than when we were. Maybe deciding what is best for them and then announcing it was not the best option.

So instead of seeing our primary role as parents, as deciding what was best for our kids and then telling them what to do, these are some alternative roles we have adopted:

- **Imagineer** - Artists create a picture of what's possible. Something we could not imagine. Us parents can do the same with our kids. Not in a manipulative way ("I know you could be better at math if you stopped wasting your life.") But in a way that helps them believe in a potential that they can not see yet. We have done this by calling out individual traits in our kids that we appreciate "I really like your art," "I think you're really funny, have you thought about creating an instagram account?," "I think you have an eye for photography and I'll bet people would pay you for your photos." This can also be done with team dynamics and not just individual traits. "What would it look

like if the 8 of us worked together as a team
to work on a project?"

- **Forecaster** - Parents have lived longer and
  can see patterns that kids can not. Eating lots
  of candy leads to tummy aches. Exercise
  leads to health. Sticking with a project
  instead of giving up leads to long term
  gratification. When we share these patterns
  with our kids it can be an incredible
  advantage.

ONE WORD OF CAUTION: Parents having an
understanding of patterns is NOT a replacement
for kids arriving at a conclusion themselves. The
best role for parents is NOT to give kids their
conclusions but to HELP children arrive on their
own. For this we have found it most helpful to ask
questions. NOT just manipulate statements with a
question mark at the end but *actual* questions.
How do you feel after watching TV all day? What
would *you* like to see more of in your life?

- **Administrator, Servant** There are many
  more roles parents can play including the
  most important - **The Example**, which we'll
  talk about later. The goal here is just to show
  that there are alternative roles to the

common traditional, power based, leadership which is giving orders and expecting obedience OR the just-as-ineffective-cousin - complete passive detachment, "you live your life, and I'll live mine" forms of parenting.

Back at home, it was 2pm. Kami, I and the 6 kids, ages 4-18, were gathered around the dining room table. "We have an idea that we want to share with you guys. We think this will be interesting to you and we want to invite you guys to give feedback on a plan that we've created. Then, you can decide if you want to be a part of it."

Our kids have learned that just because something was optional does not mean it's not important. We had given them the option of opting out of many activities in our family from hiking the Appalachian Trail, to running and training for marathons, to school. So they knew we were serious when we said it was just our idea. They had also learned to listen carefully because many of the best things in our lives came in this same form.

"Everyone's life right now is completely different and changed. This creates an incredible opportunity for us to reassess our schedule and prioritize our life. If we do what will naturally happen, we will be doing what is easiest but not necessarily what is the most rewarding. So, we want to present you guys with an idea that we could try out for one week."

"You guys will be invited to be a part of it, and for the next week our family will be prioritizing our resources in this direction."

"We would like to help you guys figure out what *you* want to do and help you guys do *that*. The things you're the most proud of doing. Those things you think will help you in the long-run."

We have found it's natural to speak to kids like they are below you. The tone of voice and words we often use indicate that they are dumber, lesser beings. But we have found speaking to our kids just like they are adults causes them to respect us and themselves more and results in more trust.

Then we wrote the schedule up on the chalkboard.

7:15 - 7:50	AM Workout
8:00 - 9:00	Breakfast/Quiet Time
9:00 - 10:00	Work Block 1
10:00 - 10:15	Break
10:15 - 11:15	Work Block 2
11:15 - 11:30	Break
11:30 - 12:30	Work Block 3
12:30 - 1:15	Lunch
1:15 - 2:15	Work Block 4
2:15 - 4:00	Break
3:00 - 3:30	Chores
4:00 - 5:30	Running
6:00 - 7:00	Dinner / Sharing Time
8:00 - 9:00	One Episode of TV series
10:00	Go to bed

We could see Eden (17) get instantly excited. She craves structure and was our one child that elected to go to public school. We asked if anyone had any feedback.

Eden asked if Saturdays would be the same. This was typically our rest day. We told her we had no plans on changing Saturdays as our rest day. Then she asked if Friday was going to be a regular movie, like we normally did or if it was going to be an episode of a TV show?

We have come to believe that ALL feedback is important. Every question or statement made by every age contains an expression of their reality that is important for us to accept, listen to, and attempt to understand. Our children have concerns, fears, and values that often come out in funny ways that are hard to understand. To dismiss a question or statement just because we don't understand it is to dismiss the person speaking the statement.

One of the goals of getting feedback is to hear ideas we couldn't think of ourselves. We didn't have the one, right answer. The only right schedule is the one we can all agree on, so feedback from the kids is not just a kind gesture, it's a necessity. The second reason we ask for feedback, is we have seen that offering space for feedback, even if none is given, helps kids feel a sense of ownership over the plan. They accept it as theirs. Something that they adopted instead of an outside force that was put upon them. This is key when it comes to carrying the plan out later on. It can be tempting to skip this stage or to just enforce edicts from on high. I've adopted a quote I read years ago:

"There are two kinds of people in the world. There are lovers and there are workers. And lovers will always get more work done."

-Tim Keller

If there is a way to get our kids to fall in love with the task at hand, to believe that it is in their best interests, to get them to want it, to get them to choose it, we will far surpass the results of forcing them to do things that we think are best. For true love to happen, they must see the task as theirs. They must own it.

Sometimes we spend so much time enforcing our plans that we suck at the art of making a plan appealing to begin. If making a plan is step one. Step two is selling it. The best invitations have gold foil and speak of fancy meals and drinks. They draw you in. Invitations are an art. They sell the event. They don't require you to be there, but they make you feel like if you're not there, you'll be missing out.

Instead of spending energy forcing our kids to do things, what if we spent our energy making the event so beneficial and helpful for our kids that it's irresistible? Our kids are smarter than we think and they want what's best for them too. Sometimes it's just difficult to see what that is. What a privilege to have some ideas that we can share and then partner with them on the same goal.

Now that we had the schedule, we still had the hard part ahead of us. The kids were not bought in yet. There were four one-hour time blocks scheduled for each day but no one knew what those work blocks were. I had the feeling that whatever we put in them would be the determining factor in the kids being willing to buy in. This was our most crucial step.

RELEASING PURPOSE IN YOUR KIDS

Every American has a bucket list. A list of grand activities they hope to accomplish someday.

- Skydiving.

- Visiting all the national parks

- Writing a book

- Retiring on the beach

Sometimes our bucket lists are spoken out loud but often they remain in our subconscious as a hope or expectation...a fantasy. But the thing that all bucket list items have in common is their timeline....*someday*. They are future events. What's better than someday? NOW! Sorry, I didn't mean to shout. Now, now, now, now, now.

So many people have written about the dangers of someday I don't want to get into it, but here's a sample.

- "Someday never comes" - CCR

- In the 4-hour Workweek, Tim Ferris wrote about practicing mini-retirements early on in your life because so many folks were getting to their traditional retirement and realizing that they were bored and actually didn't enjoy the activities and lifestyle that they had spent their whole life postponing and sacrificing for.

The bottom line is that your bucket list should be a weekly event instead of a once of a lifetime goal. There's so many things we can't control about someday, and so many things we can control about now. "Someday" is an excuse. The problem with the bucket list isn't the activity, it's the timeline. Take the examples from above:

- Skydiving.

- Visiting all the national parks

- Writing a book

- Retiring on the beach

Not all of these events are feasible now. But that doesn't mean we need to ignore our goals and commit our hours and dollars to someone else's goals continuing to live out of panic cycles, while we wait for retirement! Instead of ignoring our bucket list items for "someday," what if we were to write down what each of these activities represent? *Why* we want to do them? We might come up with something like this.

- Skydiving.
  - Adventure
  - Risk taking
  - Facing Fears

- Visiting all the national parks
  - Outdoor activities
  - Seeing beauty
  - Exercise

- Writing a book
  - Sharing my voice
  - Practicing my art
  - Finding Confidence

- Retiring on the beach
  - Relaxation
  - Self-care
  - Prioritize my own values

Now, we have something we can work with. In fact we can just get rid of our original bucket list items altogether. Who needs them? Then we'll end up with this list.

- Adventure
- Risk taking
- Facing Fears
- Outdoor activities
- Seeing beauty
- Exercise
- Sharing my voice
- Practicing my art
- Finding Confidence
- Relaxation
- Self-care
- Prioritize my own values

Each of these items can be planned into your next week! How could you plan adventure into your life right now? How would you practice sharing your voice this week? This list can create action now. And I'll bet if you're not willing to plan adventure now, you're not going to like it when you're 60 either.

Now keep in mind. This started with a generic list. I hope you make your own. But even if you just use the list above your life would probably be exponentially happier if you started to plan just 15 minutes a week of each of these activities into their life right *now*. It would take 3 hours!

This may seem like a tangent but when we asked our kids about scheduling 4 hours of "work" into their life a day *these* are the things we're talking about. It's called work because it's hard. But just because it's work doesn't mean it needs to suck. Work spent achieving the things you care about is just as valid as work spent doing things you're "supposed to do" or that your boss cares about.

This list can be hard for some and requires quite a bit of imagination because from a very young age we are taught that what you care about does not matter unless it is a weekend or you are 60. Another way to arrive at some answers is to imagine what you would do in a week if you won the lottery. Not the first week. Subtract the jet skis, and trip to the Bahamas and Netflix till your eyes bled but after all the newness wore off what would you do? Most people don't think about it seriously.

For our family members, I had written a list of ideas based upon my goals, our house, and what I knew of our kids.

We wrote it on the chalkboard.

- Take pictures with the drone
- Record a podcast
- Film a Vlog Episode
- Sell something on eBay
- Build something
- Learn something
- Edit something
- Publish something
- Build a website
- Create some merch
- Write a letter
- Take some photos
- Fix something (our front door hadn't worked in 3 weeks)
- Take an online course
- Watch a YouTube tutorial
- Create art
- Landscape the yard
- Plant some seeds
- Weed garden
- Paint a room
- Clean the basement
- Create a photo book
- Write a book (my goal for how *this* book would be written)
- Learn a recipe
- Create a healthy meal plan
- Create an Instagram page
- Write a song
- Record a song
- Practice an instrument

The kids added to the list...

- Practice dancing
- Film video course
- School work (Eden's school was not meeting but still had assignments)
- Learn storytelling
- Help neighbor
- Remodel room
- Launch merch store
- Build bunny cage

I even posted my goal on Facebook and other people shared what they wanted to do by Friday:

- I want to finish one drawing.
- I want to have the demo mess cleared out of our flip house so we can have H-VAC in next weekend.
- We want to hike at least 5 more miles this week, as a family.
- I want to get the boxes unpacked from the move and get organized.
- I want to get out and walk at least three times this week.
- I want to have three solar panels mounted on my trailer .

- I want to learn to play a song on the fiddle.
- Have a grandkid sleepover.
- Practice 4 to 5 hours a day and spend at least an hour of that time each day practicing double tonguing! (from a professional saxophone player).
- Publish my coaching website and fine-tune a Beatles song on piano.

As you can see, there are no wrong answers.

We paused and asked again, "If you could do anything or learn anything, that you'd be excited about, what would it be?" This was it. Our list was done for now, but always open to be added to.

Now it was time for the invitation. "How many of you would like to be involved in a schedule where you get to prioritize your own values in a structured way for one week?"

Eden (17) raised her hand before I finished the sentence.

Memory (13) quickly followed by raising her hand, "I do."

"Me," said Seven (15).

"I'm in," said Dove (18).

Filia (9) said "I want to do it, but I don't fully understand it."

That was ok. We were confident we could help show it to her along the way but we had unanimous buy-in from the kids and we were starting tomorrow.

FINAL DETAILS

Now that we had agreement on the schedule starting tomorrow, it was time to take care of some details. These were the things we decided were necessary to make it work.

- **Display the schedule prominently.** We have a giant chalkboard wall that we wrote our calendar on for everyone to see. Google calendar is great but there is something powerful about posting something in a public place and knowing that you all have access to it and you are all looking at the same copy. Especially with kids, we have found it valuable to post rules, schedules, and goals in a place where everyone has access. For it to be democratic it needs to be visible

- **Each person would have to put their dishes away right after the meal.** If we were going to put off cleaning until 3pm this step would minimize chaos for everyone.

- **Workspace prep.** I had been sidetracked for days by simple things like not having a garbage can or seeing too much dust on the floor. We encouraged each of our kids to take some time and decide where they want to work and prepare that space ahead of time so they're using their work block times for the goals they chose.

- **Create your own work block rules and restrictions**. Neither Kami or I wanted to be a cop and go around seeing if kids are sneaking on their phones. We have found that when we show kids *their own* goals and point out that time spent on their phones conflicts with that, they want to choose to set the phone down. This does not mean that any of us will always be successful but it changes the dynamic from cops and robbers to being allies. With the kids we created the following restrictions during our work blocks:
  - No sleep
  - No phone (we set them on the record table - a place where nothing is usually allowed)
  - No facebook
  - No Youtube
  - In general, our work blocks were scheduled for things that we valued that wouldn't, *otherwise* be prioritized. If you

would naturally do something for fun, use your work block for something else.

-

- **Schedule your goals ahead of time.** We encouraged everyone to use the 8am quiet time to plan their 4 daily work blocks so they are not using the actual time to decide.

- **Healthier meals**. As a family, we were always trying to eat healthier. We agreed that this would be a good week to try healthier meals with simpler ingredients to best fuel the larger goals you were accomplishing.

- **Computer Schedule**. We have two computers that we let the kids use. One desktop and one laptop. We created a simple schedule for the time slots.

All of these things took less than 5 minutes to communicate but were fairly important to our success. I include them here as specific examples you may deal with but also to show the role of a forecaster, servant, and administrator looks like in our family.

For our nighttime entertainment time slot, we had decided that the TV show we wanted to watch together was HBO's Westworld - the show Kami and I had watched alone the night before. We were all excited to kick our schedule off so we decided to watch the first episode that night. The show ended on a cliffhanger and we wanted to watch another but we decided to wait until tomorrow to see what would happen next.

MONDAY

THE HONEYMOON

Monday morning came and there was an excitement in the air. The first item on the schedule was 7:15 AM workout. Seven (15) and I went downstairs to the basement where the weight equipment was. It took a few minutes to find everything and set up. The girls were in the attic doing bodyweight exercises led by Dove (18). For some reason I bench pressed 115 pounds - more than I had in the last two years.

Remember, don't freak out thinking you need to start with a group exercise routine that includes your kids. This is something we had practiced for years. If you want to incorporate fitness into your goals best start with something you're familiar with. Any step forward is success and can serve as an example to others.

Normally breakfast is serve-yourself and looks like the wild west but I decided to create a communal meal to help with our schedule. I grated some potatoes for hash browns and sprinkled that with pepper-jack cheese and fried a bunch of eggs in a giant frying pan to help fuel the kids for the mission, while Kami made our coffee. The whole meal took about 20 minutes to make, was fairly healthy and cost $6.

Normally, we would spend an hour sipping coffee, writing, and reading. Now we had 30 minutes. But when it came time for our first work block there was electricity in the air. Something felt right. Something was happening that we all wanted to be a part of. Something for which it was worth skipping more coffee time.

WRITING A BOOK

It was 9am. Time for our first work block. I went up to my office and opened up a blank document. Normally this is the scariest thing to do. Normally, I'm filled with a bunch of questions. Will I finish this time or will this manuscript end up 80% done just like all the others? Will anyone read it? Who are you to think you can write a book? With only an hour to write, I didn't have much time to think of these questions. I just wrote. The first 10 pages of this manuscript were written in that first hour. This wasn't just important for me, this was important for my kids.

Eight years ago our family took a break from school for one year. That year we didn't enforce any schoolwork or lessons. Not even homeschool. We were coming off of 5 years of compulsive public school followed by classical education and homeschool models. Each one felt the same. We always felt behind and inadequate. We felt like we were letting our kids down, we felt like we were letting the world down. While on vacation I read a book called "A Thomas Jefferson Education." The book's premise was that instead of using our kids' educational years to teach them content we should teach them to enjoy and value *learning* itself. Then instead of 12 years of content - which is often followed by a hatred of learning, you will get a lifetime of content. But the most fascinating part of the book came when the question was posed "How do you create one that is passionate for learning?" There was only one way suggested. You, as the parent, must become a learner. You model it. There are no shortcuts.

Often we see the purpose of childhood as learning and the purpose of adulthood as making money. These stages just reinforce prioritizing panic. They are reactively responding to expectations put on you by the culture. We now think of learning and creativity as lifelong stages. When we do either of these things well, they create value in the world. Making money is often a byproduct of creating value but can often serve as a distraction and end up being a goal in itself that, then, cannibalizes learning and creativity. So we decided to stop focusing on money and the specific content our kids were regurgitating and started to focus on learning.

Shortly after that Kami started taking guitar lessons and I took up running. Both activities that we thought we were too old to start. It was gradual at first but the ripple effect was massive.

Eight years later 5 of our kids have learned piano, guitar, and electronic instruments. They have recorded and published their music and practiced for 1000's of hours all completely voluntarily. None of the lessons or practice was enforced. That same year Kami started taking guitar lessons, I ran my first marathon with my son Seven, who was eight at the time.

It feels too good to be true, that by prioritizing learning what *you* want to learn you are helping to model to your kids the possibility and benefits of them prioritizing their own learning. It felt like cheating. Every other educational model we had practiced all boiled down to some sort of war of the wills using an array of manipulation tactics combined with complex reward and consequence systems. And we had found that this same phenomenon of transferring passions was not only true of learning, it was true of creating. Having courage to follow my dreams of writing my book meant I was telling my children that they could write theirs.

That night, after our first day of work blocks, around a pot of Broccoli Cheddar soup that Eden (17) had made during her free time, we shared about our highs and lows as well as what we had accomplished that day.

Dove (18) said that she felt great because she had read two chapters each of three different books that she had wanted to read for a while. She had also baked two loaves of bread and been able to share some with her grandparents and had watched some tutorial videos about the settings on her camera. Seven (15) had watched drone videos on YouTube and then practiced for 30 minutes, getting footage that can be used for our family's youtube channel. Filia (9) drew some pictures she was really proud of. Her and Memory

(13) had also spent almost three hours cleaning their room and had an entire garbage bag full of trash to show for it. They were eager to take anyone on a tour that was willing. Kami and I spent our last work block hour recording a podcast that Eden published. It was a super productive day for everyone.

I shared with the kids that I had written 10 pages of my manuscript. I was so excited and it showed. I've had many ideas for books over the years and most of them rattle around in my brain as I put them off for all of the demands of *real life*. Society will never fault me for not writing my book as long as my bills are being paid, my emails are being answered and my hair is mostly combed.

But every idea that didn't get written eroded my confidence. It told me that the my ideas weren't important. And even if they were, I didn't have what it took to birth them into the world. Every idea that stayed in my head was a reminder that I'm not that special or important. That I'm just like everyone else and my greatest good was to fit in, produce money for the economy, and protect others from my craziness.

And so, when I share with my kids that I wrote 10 pages it has very little to do with the 10 pages. I am modeling that what is inside them is worth bringing to the world. I am showing them that it is possible, and I am modeling a way that it can be done. And at that dinner table we celebrated doing this together. They participated in my victory and I participated in theirs. Do you see how different this is than the placating pats on the head that we give our kids when they draw a messy flower or bring home A's on their report card? Saying "good job" about work well done is not the same as celebrating on the front lines and doing it with them. This is the power of example.

When Seven and I ran that first marathon we didn't know if we would finish, but when we crossed the finish line the rest of the kids saw it. They saw us get the medals and the free pizza and they begged to run the next one. So the next two years, Dove, Eden, and Memory joined us. They were 12, 11, and 7. And we all crossed the finish line together. By this point Filia who was 6 was begging us to come on runs because she saw all the rest of us enjoying ourselves. When it came time to run the marathon she didn't want to be left out. Kami, who never thought of herself as a long-distance runner, thought that if her 6 year old was going to try it, she may as well join. They ran their first marathon together. To date, there have been a cumulative total of 25 full marathons run by my kids not including 4 ultra marathons.

We never set out to be runners. And we never set out to write a book. These are the results of prioritizing purpose and then being willing to listen to where your inner voice is guiding. The side effects of taking your inner voice seriously can be a force to be reckoned with. All of the tasks that we finished on Monday, we accomplished on a day that we worked out, ate healthy, and ran a cumulative total of 22 miles. We were all capable of doing this 2 days before. But we didn't. Fixating on your purpose instead of letting panic take over, gets shit done.

TUESDAY

FAILURE

By the end of day two I had finished 17 pages of the manuscript. But the honeymoon had worn off and we started to notice things falling apart all over the place. Morning workout started 10 minutes later which meant breakfast got started 20 minutes later. Overall, it seems like there was less energy going into work blocks. I responded by becoming more and more of a cop and feeling the need to push the kids more. Our 15 minute breaks were feeling shorter and shorter.

I walked into the kitchen after the second work block and the kids were telling me that Kami had used her work block time to create a new profile picture on Instagram and had enlisted their help. While that somehow frustrated me, I knew that I didn't have too much space to critique.

I found myself in the middle of the third work block back to some familiar habits. I visited a few websites, which broke my "rules", and probably spent a total of 15 minutes on an unscheduled break. The old voices spoke to me. "The experiment is over." "Did you really think this was going to last forever?" "You created all this hype for a false start!" But after the 15 minutes I went back to writing.

I've learned with addictions (speaking outside of chemical addictions) that what's more addictive than specific habits (TV shows, IG feed, porn, food, web browsing) is the *shame* that surrounds its use. The shame is what says, "You suck, you don't deserve to write a book." Cupcakes don't talk. And when we face the shame, the addiction itself often goes away. Instead of feeling bad about the 15 minutes I spent surfing mindlessly I focused on a few things:

- **Maybe I needed it.** Addictions get a bad rap especially when we use terms like "coping mechanism" like it's a four letter word. Maybe I needed a break after leading a family through breakneck speeds to revamp our entire life. I had done one additional work out time and run 5 additional miles than normal and pumped out 17 pages of creative writing. Why freak out over 15 minutes?

- **Our schedule is a tool, not a prison.**
  Feeling shitty for spending 15 minutes doing something I liked instead of following "the program" is a legacy feeling from believing that my goal on earth is to serve the system. It's not. Have you heard that one Bible story where the religious teachers were freaking out about some guys doing sabbath (the rest day) wrong? Jesus' response: "Man is not here for the sabbath, sabbath is here for man." This means my damn schedule is here for me. I don't serve it. It serves me. Fuck prison. I'm a free man.

- **There's no going backwards. Everything is progress.** One of the biggest lies I tell myself is: Because I didn't get it perfect, I've somehow gone *backwards*. The effort I expended was a *waste*. There's no such thing as going backwards. It's impossible. Try going back to yesterday. You can't. Sometimes I try really, really hard to remember what it was like to be a kid and I can't do that. The same is true about remembering how I saw the world yesterday. It's impossible.

Even though I "wasted" 15 minutes, the way I see myself, the way I see my work, it's different from Sunday. I now knew I could write 17 pages in two days. I didn't know that on Sunday. And if I could write 17 pages the last two days, maybe I could write 17 pages the next two days….even it I took a 15 minute break. This new perspective meant that even though I enjoyed every "wasted" minute of my break, I found myself looking forward to getting back to the keyboard on my desk and pounding out the manuscript. 15 minutes didn't erase Sunday and Monday. If this was true of myself, it's true of my kids. Often I had created restrictions out of fear because I was concerned that my kids were not growing fast enough or maybe they were even getting dumber by playing too many video games. But fear is not a good long term-decision maker. Better to trust progress and spend that energy living as an example. The kids will see it.

No matter how hard I try and remember these things, shame is often a primary motivator and requires powerful tools to deal with. I couldn't face shame alone. Good thing for me, I didn't have to.

LEADING WITH YOUR WEAKNESS

The biggest lie that shame says, is that "you are alone." You're the only one who's failing, you're the only one who sniffs panties, you're the only one who's disappointed in themselves. I had learned in 12-step groups that this simply wasn't true. 12-Step groups - like Alcoholics Anonymous- are where people say "I'm Ben, I'm an alcoholic."

When I first started going to these groups, I heard a concept I had never heard of: "Lead with your weakness." I saw it exhibited by my sponsor, William. He had been in the program for two decades and by now you'd think he wouldn't have any problems. Week after week William would show up and share about his struggles. His struggles with failure, his struggles with human connection, and his struggles with living out his true self and potential. And every week, instead of seeing him as a loser, the other members of the group looked up to William. We found hope and encouragement in his honesty and struggle. It gave me a new perspective. Maybe some struggles would *never* go away. But just because they were there didn't mean they needed to define me. One day I asked William how he had become such a trusted leader. All he said was "lead with your weakness."

And so, at that dinner meeting where we would report on our day, I knew what I had to share. If I was going to be a leader, I would lead with my weakness.

"Today was hard. I wasted 15 minutes and felt like a failure."

Instead of laughing at me or making fun, the kids started to share about how difficult the day had been for them. Just like I had seen happen in 12-step groups, leading with your weakness shows that it's ok to be human and that none of us are the beacons of hope we see in TV advertisements, photoshopped IG pages, or positive self-help books. We're better. We're human.

Most of our parenting over the years (back when we believed it was better to be a cop) consisted of going around busting kids for spending 15 minutes online when they were *supposed* to be doing something else. When we continually busted our kids this is what happened.

1.**They got better at hiding and we got better at chasing.** *Wow*. Sounds like a great investment of resources.

2.**We shortchanged the process of them deciding that learning and creation is better than taking the easy way.** When they're always running and hiding trying to save their face they don't have energy to make a conclusion themselves. Alfie Kohn is famous for talking about studies where kids that were rewarded for being honest actually became less honest. Kids started to become more focused on the praise from adults than they did the feeling they got from being kind to someone else. When you emphasize the external it costs what's happening internally. If listening to the quiet voices inside of you and birthing those creations is actually much better than a bunch of 15 minute panic loops, than why are we so afraid that our kids won't conclude that themselves?

3.**We were training our kids to be future cops.** *Great*. Just what we needed.

We wanted to train our kids to be creators, not cops. We did this by becoming creators ourselves and letting them watch. If you're not creating yourself it will be impossible for you to inspire your kids to create. There are many ways to inspire and success is not the only one. There are a lot of failures involved in any creation. Many drunken binges, scrapped drafts, tears, second guessing, and 15 minute internet binges. So letting kids watch, means letting them watch the *entire* process, including the failures. When they see the entire process, and can share about their own feelings of failures and unmet expectations. It is when we *share* our failures that we realize that we are not alone. That is when "we are in this together" will actually mean something. Being open, being together, not being alone....*THESE* are the best tools that we have found to move right past shame on onto your first fucking draft.

WEDNESDAY

I ♥ LONG SHOWERS

Wednesday I woke up and grated three potatoes. I had learned that four was too many. Then I did an arm workout with Seven, in the basement. At 7:50 I put the potatoes on the frying pan, switched it to low and started my shower.

Normally, I put the shower to the hottest setting, sit down and end when I feel like it. I installed a tankless hot water heater with unlimited hot water and a sliding glass enclosure on the shower to maximize my comfort and minimize the variables that could reduce my shower time. On colder days, I'd fall asleep in the shower. Most of my showers are 30 minutes minimum and that's without washing my hair. I just sit there. If Kami joins me it adds 20 minutes easy. I love it. It's one of my favorite times of the day. But now there were hash browns cooking on the stove.

The hash browns are the only force strong enough to get me out of my shower. Yes, it was a sacrifice. But it wasn't just a sacrifice. One of my most blissful moments of the day was being replaced by another value: efficiency.

These sacrifices were happening all over the place. The schedule felt like a merciless master with a whip beating my freedom to a pulp. Normally I would post a picture on Facebook and watch the clicks rolling in. I could stare at the screen as the light blue boxes appeared and disappeared letting me know that someone on the planet saw my post and shared my approval. Then I would read a comment and consider engaging. Or maybe click on someone's profile who I had unfollowed and see what they were up to….only to find out they had been hanging out with someone else (who I had, also, unfollowed) but was suddenly interested in. Hours would be spent, just like at the bottom of the shower. But with 15 minute breaks in between work blocks I found myself wanting to listen to a song on my record player or jump on the trampoline with Rainier (4) instead of scroll. I still love talking long showers. But I loved that my book was getting written more. This schedule made clear, what I could see before. I couldn't have both.

As my panic loops left they were being replaced with something better. I started to wonder if I would ever feel the same familiar rush

from picking up my phone. So much had changed
and it had only been five days. I would have to
wait to find out.

THURSDAY

When I stopped acting like a cop with my kids and when I trusted that they themselves are actually motivated to create and work and do great things, I started to naturally rethink my role as a parent. Many people, who just see a snapshot of our family, equate our lack of policing to lack of care. But there are many ways to care. The foundation for the success this week had been built much earlier. If you plant a seed it doesn't matter how healthy it is if the growing environment is toxic.

In addition to the previous parenting roles we've already discussed (imagineer, forecaster, servant, administrator, and example) I'd like to introduce one other that has been key to our success. And that is the role of "Environmental Designer." A fancy way of saying parents get to choose the house, what it feels like and and the stuff with which it's filled. They say the number one variable that determines how much a kid will read when they grow up is the number of books that are in their house. Just ask any artist, writer, or teacher, the environment matters.

There are so many ways to design a home. You can do it based on what you think your guests will like. You can do it based upon a Restoration Hardware catalog. Or you can design a home based upon what you think will be the most inspirational and encourage learning and creativity. We've gone with the latter. You could use your first week of work blocks to rethink if your house is working for you, moving things, rearranging and choosing what to make more accessible and what to make less accessible. That could set you up for a lot of future weeks of living your values. I heard somewhere, "that which is keeping you from your task, is your task."

These are some things we have done to craft our environment:

- **Instruments**: We have a piano in the middle of the house. Instead of a keyboard with headphones over in the corner. All playing and practicing is a performance with an audience. We also have two guitars, a ukulele, a didgeridoo, and a bongo drum accessible at all times. When someone wants to play an instrument it is always given preference over playing music from the stereo.

- **Entertainment**: Our TV screen and theater is upstairs in the attic. Watching movies requires an active decision to go upstairs. We do not keep news or shows going on passively in the background. We do have two computers for the kids to use (one laptop and one desktop). Preference is always given to creative work and production over consumption.

- **Music:** We have recently added a record player with almost 200 vinyl records and some kick ass Bose speakers. We love to blast the music at high volumes and dance but deference is always given to those who desire silence. This is something we got from Mr. Rogers who said the preference of silence should always trump sound.

- **Garden:** We tore out a fence down between two properties and created raised garden beds that would not only grow plants but also serve as a beautiful centerpiece to the property. It is a source of peace, beauty, inspiration, food, and constant goodwork.

- **The Table**: This is the single best thing we have in our house that promotes creativity. It is a wooden slab table that is 4 feet wide and 12 feet long and it sits in our open concept dining room that is in the center of the house. We had to cut out four walls when we first moved in so it would be visible from our entire down stairs. When I was shopping for tables I looked everywhere. Ikea, Restoration Hardware, Pottery Barn and I saw the same thing. The best and biggest tables were thousands of dollars and looked "distressed." These tables told a story of hard work, heightened activity, and diversity. The problem was the story was fake. These uniform scars in the wood (usually made in Asia) had been created with electric tools to make it look like your grandparents had used this table on their farm. I knew that if we bought a table for $1,000s of dollars like this I would freak out anytime a kid wanted to draw with a sharpie, carve play-doh with a knife, or kneed 5 lbs of slime on it. Instead, a friend of mine built a table for us and we decided we were going to distress the motherfucker ourselves. The first thing we did was burn "A place to create, write and tell stories" into the bottom. Then we promptly burned a black ring on it by placing our burning hot cast iron skillet straight into the middle of it. It stands as an ode to creativity right in the middle of our house saying sharpies, slime, and woodcarving welcome. NOTE: While getting the second edition of this book ready for print my editor suggested I put the table on the cover of the book.

A few other things we have lying around our house:

- Typewriter
- Art supplies
- Books
- Adobe creative suite
- Cameras
- Cook books

For some people it would be harder than others to step out of cycles of panic. They have radios and televisions in every room that they proactively have to ignore in order to be in a creative space. We don't want to spend our energy that way. These problems can be solved by design. This week, watching the kids take full advantage of our house, the fruit of our decisions was paying off. We had our props for creativity in place. And the environment was working in cooperation with our goal.

Our property is always a work in progress and we're always looking for ways to improve and evolve. Sometimes it's a new purchase. Sometimes it's moving something distracting down to the basement. As you start on a week of change, I hope you're open to looking around and making changes that will help accomplish your goals and ask: "What is your house here for?"

FRIDAY

This was the last day of our 5 day work schedule. Coming into Friday I had written 29 pages of a manuscript. I had finished my book. It was a mini book. It was a rough and dirty book, but it was a book. I had spent 15 hours in my office (minus that 15 minutes, of course) in the course of five days, writing. It was honest, authentic, and I believe that it will help people. Even if it didn't help anyone, it helped me. It was the stuff that was inside of my head that I needed to get out. And as proud as I am of my book, that was just the tip of the iceberg.

Every day when I would come out of my office I would see what the kids were accomplishing. These are just a few of those things…

Filia (9) had learned how to make healthy smoothies and spent 3 hours cleaning out her bed and bedroom and had thrown away one garbage bag worth of trash. She had spent one morning taking pictures of flowers in the garden and learning from Memory how to edit them. She was so excited that you could brighten the colors using the saturation tool. She had watched dance tutorials and worked on her ballet moves and spent more than 10 hours drawing, using youtube tutorials.

Memory (13) helped Filia clean out their room and learned how to make Chocolate Oreo Truffles, studied percentages with her Grandma, practiced dancing, and finished numerous art projects. She had made money helping an elderly neighbor paint her door and had spent two hours mowing the lawn for the first time of the season and landscaping the yard. It was beautiful.

Seven (15) had watched drone flying technique videos and filmed drone footage for our family videos, learned how to calculate square footage and measured the area of their new house for their ongoing construction project. He also edited videos for our family vlog channel from the Appalachian Trail as well as the daily vlogs that we were publishing using Final Cut Pro. He also made dinner for the family.

Eden (16) played every song from her entire back catalog on the piano. She studied exponents with her grandma and worked on her Korean. She spent hours working on paper cut out art projects that she posts to her Instagram page and plans to sell in our merch store. She did all this while publishing vlog episodes to our families youtube channel *AND* maintaining the school work that was being assigned by her teachers.

Dove (18) had baked bread, started 3 books that her mom had recommended, watched camera tutorial videos, tried a new cookie recipe, painted a picture, and applied for jobs.

Kami paid our county business taxes, practiced her guitar for 4 hours, recorded and published multiple songs, paid out allowance to our kids, recorded a podcast episode with me for our Everyone Belongs channel, and researched shipping for Fight For Together merch - a job that only took 10 minutes but that she had been putting off for weeks.

And for me, I had logged in 19 hours working on my book. And one hour recording a podcast. The thrilling part was that it was an actual 19 hours of writing. Not the usual, five minutes of writing, five minutes of social media that I was used to. I had said at my 40th birthday party that I wanted to publish three books this year. Unrealistic?

Probably. But the worst part was that 4 months before my 41st birthday, I had given up on all of it. But, in one week I now had a book I was ready to release to the world. It was forward movement.

SPEAKING OF FORWARD MOVEMENT...

The tasks that we accomplished felt amazing and it's fun to show them off to the outside world. But they don't compare to the pride that I feel about the accomplishments that were done on the inside. Working to figure out a merch store for 10 minutes is not something that looks glorious to the outside world. But it was glorious to Kami. She faced confusion, insecurity, and paralysis and 10 minutes was a victory. It was forward movement. And this happened to every member of our family (possibly besides Filia (9) who doesn't struggle with that yet). Our kids faced their demons and they won - which is what happens *every* time that you truly face a demon. When you show up you break old patterns, you try new things, and you say no to artificial restrictions. When you show up, you win. *THIS* is what we did this week. We showed up. These were the things I was the most proud of, the things that will last forever and will transfer into every task, relationship, and journey that my kids enter into for the rest of their lives.

AND THAT'S NOT ALL

Let's not forget that as a group we watched 5 episodes of Westworld together. Some people who have much higher standards of decency (and much lower standards of nudity) will balk at our choice for a family show. That's fine. Choose your own. Our family values intense, well told stories. But for our goals the content was less important than the togetherness. Watching a common show creates common conversations and laughing points throughout the week. It creates a common language. These things are the basis of creating a common culture.

On the more difficult side, we ran a cumulative total of 110 miles. Five runs, each optional, at 5.5 miles each. It will be easy to dismiss us as crazy or extreme. If you do, that's because you're comparing yourself to us. Don't. That's when the excuses come in. "I have a bad knee and can't run." "We have 7 kids under the age of 4." Comparison to others, is a losing game. We compare ourselves to the week before. You should do the same.

Our goals are just samples. Set shorter goals, smaller goals, bigger goals, goals you can do with your kids. 15 minutes is better than nothing.

Walking with a stroller is better than sitting on the couch. Publishing during nap time is better than scrolling.

You can't control how much money you make, how many words you write, if they're any good, or if people will like them but you can show up. And when you show up the work gets done. Your demons will be faced and the more work gets done the more your work will help people. But it all starts with showing up. Remember, you're not comparing yourself with others. You're also not comparing yourself with an unrealistic and perfect ideal that doesn't exist. You're comparing yourself to reactively scrolling on Instagram, entering into panic loops, and spending your life believing that your ideas don't matter but for some reason your bosses or friend's do. Showing up and succeeding 1% is infinitely more successful than not showing up at all.

SATURDAY

For the last 10 years we have practiced a rest day. Believe it or not, it's actually one of the 10 Commandments. Right up there with not stealing and not murdering. Our religious beliefs for doing so, have changed over the years but the value has remained the same. Having a weekly time to reflect, rest, and stop from things, even when they are good can be just as important as the work itself. While we have been practicing this habit for years, this Saturday was a little different. The rest felt better, more special. Like we had earned it. The longer you walk the more you enjoy sitting.

Some things we've learned from 10 years of proactive rest:

1. **Resting breaks up monotony**. Working is great. Working without ending is not. This week, every day started to feel the same. It's easy to feel like we're in a video game or on a hamster wheel. These feelings make creativity suffer. They lower our energy. They

flatten our point of view.

2.Rest reminds us that we are not our work.
It's great to do good work. But it's not great
to think you are your work. To think that
when your work is going great *you* are doing
great and when your work is going bad, *you*
are doing bad means that your work has too
much power. It has taken over your life. This
is bad for you and this is bad for your work.
The better the work the more important it is
to take a break from it.

3.A rest day puts production in its place. We
are not machines. We are humans. We
dance, we enjoy flowers. These "non-
productive" activities are no less important
than work and deserve just as much
prioritization. Production and creation are
just a few of the wonderful things we do. The
art we look at, the music we listen to, and the
relationships that we enjoy are just as
valuable.

How do we celebrate? (We start our celebration at dinner time on Friday night and go to dinner on Saturday night)

- We drink beer.
- We smoke cigars.
- We cook a fancy meal or order pizza or Chinese.
- We light candles.
- We drink cherry coke (a bad habit we picked up while hiking the A.T.).
- We watch a movie together and eat candy.
- We sleep in.
- We make waffles or get donuts.
- We make fresh-squeezed orange juice.
- We drink more coffee.
- We read, paint, watch YT videos to do whatever the fuck we want.
- We wear our pajamas all day.
- We smoke cigars, again.
- Kami and I take a shower together.
- We have the best sex of our week.
- Then we go out to dinner and a bookstore.

Basically we break all the rules. They were made up anyways.

SUNDAY

REASSESSMENT

Seven days ago I had an idea. I met with Kami to share that idea with her and get her feedback. This set in motion a process that got a best selling book written and a bunch of other wonderful things. But it would be an error to sit back and assume that we had created a masterpiece and could spend the rest of our lives implementing and selling this process. People change, machines break, and that's ok. The goal is to move *forward*, not be *finished*.

Creativity is not black or white. There's no on/off switch. The same applies to addictive panic loops. We've come to see them as big round dials on the dashboard we call life. The dials go from one to ten. But you can only have so many turned up at a time because our energy is limited. Sometimes the dials don't get turned for a long time. Sometimes they get stuck. But maturity and evolution is a constant process of figuring out which ones you want up and down depending on the day and week.

At the beginning of this week, partially due to the coronavirus, I would say our panic dial was at an 8. "Things are closing, this is scary, stay home" was the only thing we could hear. Our Creativity dial was at one. We were trying to turn the panic dial down but couldn't figure out how. Facebook's algorithm was playing off our fear and not helping us. That dial was stuck.

Things are closing, this is scary, stay home.
Things are closing, this is scary, stay home.
Things are closing, this is scary, stay home.

But we learned that we *could* control the creativity and production dials. We cranked those up to 9. For a while it felt like we were gonna break. But then a funny thing happened.

It was during a break on Thursday after writing page 25 of this manuscript that I opened up youtube and saw a new video was posted. "Logan Paul Done Dirty." It was surrounded by "'People Are Dying': Battling Coronavirus Inside a N.Y.C. Hospital" and "Bill Gates makes a prediction about when coronavirus cases will peak". Honestly, I was the most interested in the Logan Paul one, but none of them had the same appeal they did, just five days earlier. *Then*, I would have clicked instantly. Why not? Compared to boredom consuming videos seem like great options. But, I wasn't bored anymore. Because of what we had been through with our chalkboard, seeing the kids, and spending 15 hours writing, I was caught up in bringing my idea to the world. Compared to bringing the greatness inside of us into the outside world now these videos seemed kind of silly. They seemed like distractions. The dial was loose. And when the dials are loose I can turn them wherever. Now, in place of the old panic loop - Things are closing, this is scary, stay home - it felt like there was new propulsion in our life: "You can do it, what you want is valuable, one step at a time." While the old panic loop resulted in paralysis and discouragement. This new perspective felt motivating *and* empowering.

You can do it, what you want is valuable, one step at a time.

You can do it, what you want is valuable, one step at a time.

You can do it, what you want is valuable, one step at a time.

PERSPECTIVE

We hiked the 2,200 mile Appalachian Trail as a family and I don't care if my kids ever hike one mile again. But, I love that they know they *can* do it if they choose to. We just finished a massive week of productivity. And I don't care if my kids ever do it again. But one lesson they took away, that they can't unlearn is that they *can* do it if they choose to.

Kami said that the new chore schedule was the most effective of anything she had tried in eight years. By prioritizing her own creativity and trusting the kids, it changed the way we all saw the work around the house.

So not only did we get the communal health from running and eating better, combined with the better environment that we were living in (cleaner rooms, landscaped and mowed yards), and the songs we had written, the videos we had edited, the books we had written, the skills we had built - we had something that would literally impact the entire rest of our life. We had a new way of seeing our house. We had a new way of seeing our capabilities.

We all got a vantage point that we can not unsee. So when we go back to regular life I don't need to worry about my children forgetting and losing everything. They know the feeling of baking bread, mowing the lawn, having a clean room, and for me, writing my book. So, if I get to a point where the panic dial gets turned up, I may live in it for a while. But when I do, I'll be living in it with the awareness that there is another option out there. And *this* is one of the best gifts I think we can ever give our children. This is the gift of parenting.

The way you see yourself affects what you do. If you see yourself as a helpless victim that is subject to a disaster happening on the other side of the globe, or the panic happening outside of your front door, or on twitter what you do will be based upon those limitations. But if you see yourself as a free person, free to go on Instagram or free to sit down with a pencil and paper and look inside of yourself to see what it is you really care about and you know that no one needs to give you permission to go and do those things, you can start today. You can start forward movement. And that is all I can ask for.

And so, one week later, on Sunday Kami and I celebrated. We also shared:

- What skills we learned?

- What we learned about ourselves?

- If we wanted to set any new goals for the next week?

Our next week will be different, will it be better? Maybe, maybe not. It will be based upon what we learned and it will be more of what I want and less of me responding to the panic that's around me. And for me, that's a better week. And better weeks lead to better lives.

We started off this week being driven by panic. There is a global pandemic that is outside of our control. It consumed hours of our day but produced nothing In investor language there was no ROI (return on investment). The more we fought the panic the worse it got. We felt like shit. Because not only was the fear of the actual disease weighing on us, but our lack of discipline with no hope of change. Instead of viewing this cultural state as a curse, we saw it as an opportunity to understand the responsive panic that governs our lives most of the time. Normally it's just more difficult to see. And after just one week we had found a solution that could help us far beyond the lockdown. Very simply, our solution was to make room for the pieces of our lives that we always believed were special but were not prioritizing. And in the course of doing that, we noticed many of the panic cycles had gone away. The world was still on fire and the news was still reporting but we didn't have the void to fill anymore.

If you have found yourself living in a play, fulfilling someone else's dreams, or caught in cycles that, at the end of the day, you don't really care about. My guess is your kids are heading in the same direction. And if you can lead them, and yourself in a different direction, it could change your life...or at least your week.

Let's go.

DID THIS BOOK HELP?

We'd love to hear about it.

The absolute BEST WAY:

Honest reviews help readers find the right book for their needs.We'd appreciate a review on amazon!

Tag is in your pictures, quotes and schedules so she can see them and cheer you on!

Instagram
@fightfortogether
#familyunleashed

Thank you.
- Ben

WHERE TO FIND US

....

YouTube: Fight for together

Instagram: @fightfortogether

Facebook: fight for together

Merch: fightfortogether.bigcartel.com

COMING SOON

Ben writes about walking 2,200 miles with angsty teenagers and a screaming toddler. Together, the family faces snowstorms, record-breaking heat, facing sickness and the most difficult challenge: each other.

Ben shares what the family learned by stepping away from all of the conveniences and comforts that life has. He also shares about the beliefs that allowed them to pursue their ultimate dream of walking from Georgia to Maine on the Appalachian Trail.

Coming Summer 2020.

ADDITIONAL RESOURCES

Unconditional Parenting: Moving from Rewards and Punishments to Love and Reason by Alfie Kohn

Alfie Kohn is one of the few people I have found who writes about the dangers of short term rewards and consequences. He also has a DVD lecture with the same title that is very good

Hold On to Your Kids: Why Parents Need to Matter More Than Peers by Gabor Maté

Dr. Maté explains how crucial it is and why it is so difficult that parents fight to remain the primary influencers in their children's lives.

Do Schools Kill Creativity? by Sir Ken Robinson

My favorite TED talk of all time that gives another take on education, trusting kids, allowing them to make mistakes, and releasing creativity

Family Business: A book about Patagonia's Innovative On-Site Childcare by Malinda Chouinard and Jennifer Ridgeway

This book is one of my favorite parenting books with great examples of how to craft contexts for growth especially for young ages.

The War of Art by Steven Pressfield

The single most empowering and inspirational book I've read when it comes to creating art.

A Million Miles in a Thousand Years: How I Learned to Live a Better Story by Donald Miller

This book really helped me ask questions about whether or not we were living the type of story that was worth writing about and gave me a framework for finding purpose and finding adventures.

One Week Family Quarantine Bootcamp

Our video series from this week that's on our YouTube Channel

How to Talk So Kids Will Listen & Listen So Kids Will Talk by Adele Faber A classic about communication

with smaller people.

Selfish Reasons to Have More Kids: Why Being a Great Parent is Less Work and More Fun Than You Think

I love this book because of it's chapters on twin studies. It shows that much of the work we put into parenting doesn't change the outcome of the kids

To the Treeline

Documentary about our family setting the record to be the largest family to hike the Appalachian Trail. Just one example of what purpose can look like

Our Family Running a marathon with Filia when she was 6

Mentioned this in the book and it's a great example of one of the most difficult purpose driven activities we've undertaken

Entrepreneuring the Homefront

A Three-part video series we did talking about the importance of a weekly schedule.

All links and videos available at fightfortogether.com

With Gratitude

Joe Harold, Ashlee Mello, Sarah Freihaut and "Ed" who provided early feedback on my ghetto google doc.

Tim Vogt who's feedback was instrumental in helping me bring the hero back home.

Em Sites Karnes IG who created our first cover with 10 minutes notice and a 2 hour deadline @electric.lady.em

Christine Wilson who edited the hell out of this, made it less cringy, and gave me confidence that maybe I am a writer and gave us the idea for the cover.

And Dove for using work block #1 to help me take a picture for the new cover.

 **Ben Crawford** played blackjack professionally for 10 years before founding an internet startup company where he served clients like Google and Facebook.

He retired from corporate jobs to spend time with his family and travel. He records video and podcasts for Fight For Together and Everyone Belongs.

In 2018 he led his family to be the largest family to hike the 2,200 mile Appalachian Trail.

He lives with his wife and 6 kids in Bellevue, KY.